Newlyn And Its Pier

Wladislaw Somerville Lach-Szyrma

In the interest of creating a more extensive selection of rare historical book reprints, we have chosen to reproduce this title even though it may possibly have occasional imperfections such as missing and blurred pages, missing text, poor pictures, markings, dark backgrounds and other reproduction issues beyond our control. Because this work is culturally important, we have made it available as a part of our commitment to protecting, preserving and promoting the world's literature. Thank you for your understanding.

Newlyn and its Pier.

BY

REV. W. S. LACH-SZYRMA, M.A.,

VICAR OF NEWLYN S. PETER.

1884.

PENZANCE:
PRINTED BY F. RODDA.

PREFACE.

The following little history has been written at the suggestion of one of the Vice Presidents of our West Cornwall Fisheries Exhibition, who thought that strangers would wish to know something about Newlyn and its Pier; and also that the inhabitants might desire to be informed about the history of their native place. I must crave the indulgence of my readers, as the subject of a description of events, in some of which I have been an actor, is extremely difficult, and also that the time given me for accumulating information has been so very limited.

The profits of the sale of this little statement, after paying the expenses of publication, will be given to the Newlyn Pier Fund.

W. S. LACH-SZYRMA.

NEWLYN AS IT WAS.

HISTORY.

The authentic history of Newlyn begins, as this our little account must end, with the pier. The first mention of Newlyn in authentic records is the appeal of Edmund Lacy, Bishop of Exeter in 1435. "To all who should contribute toward the repairing and maintaining of a certain key or jetty at Newlyn, in the Parish of Paul."

What the history of the little town was before then it would be vain to enquire. Perhaps it hardly existed. All we can say is that tradition represents the shore in the olden time to have extended where tolerably deep sea is now, that all or most of Gwavas Lake was once a low country near the sea (probably like the low country by Gulval), that there close to the ocean where now the pier is to be built, a town was built which in time was submerged by the waves and buried under the encroaching (still encroaching) waters of Gwavas Lake.

If we accept this theory, we can easily explain the name of Newlyn which would be merely the Newpool or the pool recently formed where land once was by the encroachment of the sea. If so the buried town may not be mythical, for it is most probable that from the earliest time when the shores of Mount's Bay were peopled, some cottages or huts existed near this, its western end.

The conversion to Christianity of the west side of Mount's Bay, and the final establishment of a Christian church was probably the work of the great Breton bishop and missionary, St. Pol-de-Leon, in whose honour it is probable that our Paul Feast is kept up at Newlyn, Mousehole, and Paul churchtown in October.

At the time of the Norman Conquest this part of the shores of Mount's Bay belonged it seems to Alward, hence it appears in the Domesday book as Alwareton. If this be the case, and if Alverton be really the original title of this district, *i.e.* of Penzance and Newlyn,—the manor on the north shore of Mount's Bay (certainly including some territory now under water, and probably a good deal of the water we wish to enclose now in our Newlyn harbour), then we have in Domesday a rough account of the population here. It had been taxed at two but was really three hides of land. Of arable land there were sixty caracutes. In the domain three caracutes.

The population included eleven bond servants (a sad memorial of the days when bondage or serfdom existed in West Cornwall, as indeed throughout Europe), with thirty-five "villains" (the old term for a villager), twenty-five borderers.

If Newlyn existed then we cannot say, but the next event which happened to Paul parish worthy of note was the bestowal of the patronage of the benefice by the famous Richard, Earl of Cornwall, King of the Romans, son of King John, to the monastery of Hailes, in Gloucestershire.

The parish of Paul had then a definite existence and

as we have seen, in the reign of Henry VI., Newlyn was an established fishing town with a small pier for its ships and fishing boats.

The first account we have of Gwavas Lake is from William of Worcester, who visited St. Michael's Mount in 1478, and says very truly " the chef rode of the bay for seemen that cometh this way is called Gooveslake." In modern English "the chief roadstead of the bay for seamen that come this way is called Gwavas Lake." This is the contention of our Newlyn Harbour Commissioners, for we consider the Gwavas Lake region of the bay to be the safest roadstead for seamen who come this way, and so we want to give them a good pier and a safe harbour of refuge for small craft sheltered from W.S.W. and S. and N. winds. It is curious that William of Worcester should have noticed this truth 400 years ago, at a time too, when, as the land must have extended further south than now, the case was less strong than at present.

Leland in the reign of Henry VIII (as the King's Antiquary) visited Newlyn and describes it thus: "Newlin is a poore fishar towne and hath alonly a key for shippes and bootes with a lytle socur of land water" *i.e.* the Tolcarn river. He confused Newlyn and Mousehole in saying there was a little low island near Newlyn quay. He likewise says like William of Worcester, "also in the bay is a good road for ships called Gwavas Lake." He tells us that there is a chapel in the town of Penzance as was the case in Newlyn, for their parish churches — Madron and Paul — were more than a mile off. So there was a chapelry in Newlyn, just as at St. Mary's Penzance. The site of it is uncertain, tradition points to near Trewavas street.

It would seem as if Leland made Newlyn his headquarters for a few days, for he writes in his description "from St. Just to Newlin eastward the ground is somewhat hilly, &c.," " also in the S.W. point, betwixt St. Just and Newlyn, is Castle Trevyne (Treryn.)" Again he says, " betwixt the southwest and Newlyn is St. Buryan ;" also he says " the country from Newlyn to Helston is metely (fairly) fertile." So it would appear as if Leland made his excursions from Newlyn and lodged here. He tells us that Kiwarton was the chief person at Newlyn. Is this a sort of slip for Keigwin?

Leland is very positive on "there hath been much land devoured of the sea betwixt Penzance and Mousehole. An old legend of St. Michael speaketh of a townlet in this part now defaced and lying under water." To this legend we have referred, and to it possibly the town may owe its name New-Lyn—the new pool.

The most memorable event in the history of Newlyn occurred in the reign of Queen Elizabeth, in July 23rd, 1595. The Spaniards that morning under Don Diego de Brochero, burnt Mousehole and Paul church, leaving but the old manor house of the Keigwins (now the Keigwin Arms) in Mousehole, and the tower and an arch in Paul church. The four gallies sailed round Penlee point and advanced on Newlyn. Here they landed their troops. The Spanish soldiers ascended the hill at the back of the town and formed in order of battle, sending out skirmishers. Not seeing any armed resistance except the small band of Sir Francis Godolphin, they descended the hill and advanced towards Penzance. Newlyn was taken and burnt, apparently without resistance. Sir Francis retired before them on the Western Green. Here the artillery from the galleys opened fire on the Cornish who were greatly shaken by it. "Some," Carew says, "fell flat on the ground and others ran away." Sir Francis tried to make a stand at the Market place. The Spaniards however entered Penzance in three places and having taken the town burnt it as well as Newlyn.

The burning of Newlyn must have destroyed all the old town, of which no relic remains. What became of the inhabitants we cannot tell. James of Newlyn was killed, the rest probably fled into the country—they had time to get away, for the alarm at Mousehole, and the burning of that place and Paul must have occupied some hours.

On July 24th, the Spaniards made a reconnaisance, but re-embarked and moved their ships further off from the shore. On July 25th, help having arrived at Marazion from Plymouth, and Drake sailing with his ships round the Lizard, the Spaniards made off. This was the only successful landing of the Spanish troops on British soil in spite of the vast efforts of Philip II. The last cruize of Drake in defence of his country, was on behalf of Penzance and Newlyn. He afterwards sailed to the West Indies, and a few months later died and was buried in the deep.

In the period of the civil wars, we have a characteristic account of the state of society here in the journals of Mr. Daniel of Laregan, who in simple narrative relates some of his troubles here when Fairfax's troops took Penzance.

At this period the Old Cornish language must have been dying out at Newlyn, which, with Mousehole, was its last stronghold. This language was a Celtic tongue, quite distinct from the English, and more like the Breton and the Welsh, than any other living European languages. It once was spoken, not only throughout Cornwall, but also in the South Hams of Devon and throughout the Tamar Valley. It gradually became superseded by English until in the seventeenth century, however, it was almost confined to Newlyn, Mousehole, St. Just, and the neighbourhood of the Lizard. It seems that the Newlyn people gave it up before those of Mousehole, (which thus claims to be the death place of an European language; and, perhaps, the only such death-place known in Europe.) The last sentence of Cornish used in Newlyn, which people still living remember, was the fisherman's cry: "*Breal meta truja peswartha, pempthez, whethez all is scrawed.*" *Breal* is mackerel (the striped fish,) *meta* second, *truja* third, *peswartha* fourth, *pempther* fifth. The numerals, as remembered by a few of our old people, who learnt them in childhood, were :—

1 UN.	8 EITH.	15 PEMPTHACK.
2 DU.	9 NAU.	16 WHETHACK.
3 TRI.	10 DEIG.	17 SEITHACK.
4 PADZHER.	11 UNJACK.	18 EITHACK.
5 PEMP.	12 DORTHACK.	19 NAUNJACK.
6 WHETH.	13 TRITHACK.	20 IGANS.
7 SEITH.	14 PESWARTHACK.	

A considerable number of words, perhaps about 200, are however, still retained in use from the Cornish language, *e.g.*, AREE—exclamation of wonder; BAL—a mine; MORGY—a sea dog or dog fish (MOR—sea, GY—dog); PADZI POW—a lizard; PIGGY WIDDEN—little white one (term of endearment to children); CLUNK—to swallow, &c.; MURRIAN—Ants, &c. The accent also of the Cornish people is, as will be noticed by an intelligent stranger, distinct from the accent of the Anglo-Saxon people, and more akin to that of the North French; the words are spoken syllabically with a slight intonation at the end of each sentence.

The chief works on the Cornish dialect, are Miss L. Courtney's valuable Glossary and Dr. Jago's work.

Those who wish to know something of the ancient tongue should see Williams' "Lexicon Cornu-Britannicum," or Norris' Grammar; also "Lluyd" and what is called "Price's Grammar" are valuable. The literature of old Cornish was mainly dramatic, the "Origo Mundi," the "Passio Christi," the "Resurrection," Ascension," and "Death of Pilate," have been printed, as well as the "Beunans Meriasek." West Cornish people were as fond of the drama in the middle ages as now.

The history of Newlyn in the latter half of the last century, mainly gathers around the missionary efforts of John Wesley, and his visits to this place. No writer of the last century speaks so much of Newlyn, and illustrates the state of society there as much as Rev. John Wesley.

According to his own statements in his journal, it would appear, though he visited St. Ives and St. Just in 1743, yet his first sermon at Newlyn was in 1747. He describes it thus, and doubtless his own words will be valued. "Hence," *i.e.* from Zennor, "I rode to Newlyn, a little town on the south sea, about a mile from Penzance. At five I walked to a rising ground near the sea shore, where was a smooth white sand to stand on." (Where could that place have been? Was it the place where the landslip occured between Street-an-Nowan and Newlyn cliff, which has been so changed since?) "An immense multitude of people was gathered together, but their voice was as the roaring of the sea. I began to speak and their voice died away."

His next visit was in 1748 (next year.) He again seems to have ridden over from Zennor. He says, "I reached Newlyn a little after four. Here was a congregation of quite another sort, a rude, gaping, staring, rabble rout, some of whom were throwing dirt and stones continually. But before I had done all were quiet and still, and looked as if they felt what was spoken."

Next year it seems he did not visit Cornwall, but on his 7th itinerary in 1750, he wrote, under August 17, "I preached at Newlyn in the evening. Through all Cornwall I find the societies have suffered great loss from want of discipline." Wisely said the ancients, the soul and body make a man; the spirit and discipline make a Christian. This remark of Wesley on Newlyn and Cornwall is still worthy of consideration.

In his eighth visit to Cornwall he again visited Newlyn, and was disturbed by a storm, and a vehement shower of rain and hail, " but the bulk of the congregation stood quite still, every man in his place." Sept. 8, 1751.

In 1753, July 30, on his next visit, Wesley was again unfortunate, for he was taken ill with headache. For a day or two he was quite an invalid. His sermon was on " Except your righteousness shall exceed the righteousness of the Scribes and Pharisees, ye shall in no case enter the kingdom of heaven."

In 1758 he came again, and remarked on a case of sudden death, which he turned to account, preaching on the words " There is no work, nor device, nor knowledge, nor wisdom in the grave whither thou goest."

His work at Newlyn seems to have been appreciated.

In 1757 (Sept. 11) he preached at Newlyn to a large

multitude. In 1760 he again preached on the cliff near Penzance (where does he mean?) and also at Newlyn, where "the storm drove us into the house,"—probably, Mr. Kelynack's, close to where the new road goes (which was destroyed recently.)

In 1762 he was more successful. He preached on the cliff and at Newlyn. "At eight, God was in the midst and many hearts were broken in pieces," he said in his quaint figurative way.

In 1765 he writes "Perceiving my voice began to fail, I resolved to preach for a while but twice a day. In the evening I preached on a little ground at Newlyn to a numerous congregation. None behaved amiss, but a young gentleman, who seemed to understand nothing of the matter."

Next year he came again, and remarked on the passing away of the old bitterness against him. He preached at Newlyn, and small rain fell all the time, but no one left. They preferred getting wet to missing the sermon. A great change must have come over the folks since then.

He was encouraged two years later also, and says "Surely God will have a people in this place, where we have so long seemed only to beat the air."

In his visit of 1770 he merely says that he preached at Newlyn.

The 14th and last visit was after nineteen years interval. Wesley was then an old man of 86. On the morning of August 21, 1789 (the year of the Great French Revolution,) he preached for the last time in Newlyn at 11 a.m., and in the evening at Penzance. "At both places I was obliged to preach abroad."

It seems from local tradition that "Mr. Wesley" was

thought a good deal of in Newlyn. The place he usually stopped at was an old thatched house near Tolcarn Mills —which was only removed lately, and might well have been preserved as a relic. I cannot but think that the old Cornish houses where Wesley stayed, or in which he preached, might well be bought up and kept. Cannot some of his followers do this? The houses are not now very many, nor would they cost much.

The Wesleyan society, which he established, took root in Newlyn, and has remained firmly fixed ever since.

The period of Wesley's last visit coincides with an epoch in the history of Europe, the Great French Revolution, which brings us down to days remembered by living persons. In 1801 the first census of Newlyn was held. In the battle of Trafalgar, and the death of Nelson—a sorrow at first overshadowing the joy of the great victory—we are brought into contact with the childhood memories of living Newlyn men.

These were the days of the press gang, and not a few stories are still current among the old people of the press gang and its doings. One old man at Tredavoe related to me how he spent nights under a hayrick for fear the horse soldiers should come and take him for a sailor (for it would seem that cavalry were used by the press gang.) An aged woman related the terror of Newlyn people rushing away from the soldiers with drawn swords, who came after the fisherman to press them into the navy. Some who went came home no more, for they were killed in battle against the French.

At one time two men-of-war entered the Bay. Soldiers were sent over the Western Green to Newlyn to close off the retreat of the sailors inland, but numbers fled to

Burian and elsewhere, and hid in the mines. Boats came over from the ships to take the fishermen off as sailors.

Great excitement occasionally also prevailed in Newlyn by the movements of the British fleet, now and then seen in the offing. There was a gun-boat in Mount's Bay, and the Navy Inn was often the scene of frolics of the type Capt. Marryatt has so well described. The Wolf gunboat was stationed here for some time. The business of the gunboat was especially to catch privateers. In those days, it is said, that some of our fishermen who offered as privateers, really turned pirates. But this, I hope, was an antique scandal. However, tradition is in favour of the existence of "Pirates of Penzance."

In 1809 the British troops, who had to retire from Corunna under Sir John Moore, were brought in a transport to Mount's Bay. They were in a sad state after their trying expedition. This was the last defeated army that landed on Cornish shores.

Ships with French prisoners also came into the Bay, and were visited by Newlyn folk. The prisoners were sent on to Plymouth, and were lodged in Prince Town.

Towards the end of the Napoleonic wars there was some distress in Penwith. The account given by persons still living of the want of the labouring people of Newlyn in the years before Waterloo, are sad. They had hardly bread to eat, and things were very dear.

It would appear as if in the Land's End district, and indeed throughout England, the strain of the long war was bitterly felt. The salt tax was especially hard, but evaded in Newlyn, as fishermen were favoured with untaxed salt. Prices rose, seafaring men were pressed into the men-of-war, the fisheries and mercantile marine were weakened, everything was diverted to the unproductive arts of war. An old Newlyn song thus represented the Pilchard bounty:—

> "Cheer up my old men,
> Pull up my young blade,
> For the county gives bounty
> For the pilchard trade."

We cannot wonder at the general joy which gathered around the Peace, or the festivities which marked it. An effigy was made of the Emperor Napoleon I., with a scroll "I can do no more for you," and put in a boat and then taken to Mousehole Island, where it was burnt. Triumphal arches were made, and young girls, in white dress, with pink and blue sashes, danced in honour of the event. A public tea was given at the expense of the gentry *al fresco*, on the shores of the bay. Some of the Newlyn fishermen, who were away at Plymouth, took part in the famous pageant of the "Dockyard walking," in honour of the Peace. They bore appropriate marks of their calling, nets, &c.

In those days, and for some years after, the high duties encouraged smuggling among the fishing population. It would seem, however, that not so much was carried on at Newlyn itself, as might be supposed, for Prussia Cove was the smugglers head quarters, and here Mount's Bay smugglers had their rendezvous in a quieter spot than under the lee of the gunboat in Newlyn. Some of the smuggling stories are curious, but relate to remoter parts of Penwith, where the preventive men were less busy than in Newlyn.

Some years after Waterloo, the fish tithes were

found very oppressive, and riots occured. The fish tithes were afterwards abolished.

In 1848, the need of the formation of Newlyn into a separate parish was felt, and a new parish was therefore cut out of Madron and Paul. The first vicar of St. Peter's was the Rev. George Edmund Carwithen, B.A., of Jesus College, Cambridge. The first temporary church was the building called the Reading Room, in Newlyn town. The church was gazetted on March 3rd. Mr. Carwithen was incumbent until 1851, when he joined the Royal Navy as chaplain, and afterwards served with credit in divers important posts. He died only a few months since, much respected.

The second incumbent was Rev. J. H. Stockham, who was succeeded in 1856 by Rev. John Pope Vibert, who for 17 years was incumbent, and to whose energy and devotion Newlyn owes the erection of St. Peter's Church.

Mr. Vibert was a Penzance man by birth, and was greatly esteemed by all who knew him.

The question of a pier was raised about 1870 and an order obtained, but from want of support was allowed to expire. Mr. Vibert acted for some time as secretary to the scheme. According to the proposal then made a larger harbour of refuge would have been formed, than is now intended, *i.e.*, from Tolcarn to the Green Rocks. The present scheme was started in 1882, and a committee appointed, of which the Vicar was chairman, and Mr. J. Toman secretary. The committee first met in the offices of the Mount's Bay Fishing Boats Mutual Insurance Club, at Tolcarn, but afterwards at the Tolcarn Mills, until the present premises of the Harbour Commissioners were obtained close to the Foundry, where the pier and harbour business is now conducted. An important mass meeting of fishermen was held in 1884 in the Board School, over which Mr. T. S. Bolitho presided, and where a small voluntary tax on fish landed at Newlyn was agreed to.

The chief events of the last ten years in Newlyn are as follows:—

1.—The formation of the "Mount's Bay Fishing Boats Mutual Insurance Club." The need of an insurance had been long felt, indeed for 20 years, but the matter was only talked about until the almost simultaneous loss of the "Malakoff," of Newlyn (with three lives,) and the "Primitive," of Mousehole, impressed on the boat-owners the absolute need of insurance. A public meeting was held in the St. Peter's Boys' School (now used as Newlyn Institute,) and a committee appointed from Newlyn, Mousehole, and Porthleven to work out the formation of the club. This was done, and a most successful insurance society was started, and ultimately registered under the "Friendly Societies Act."

2.—Intimately connected with the Insurance Club has been the action of the Newlyn fishermen, relative to the Board of Trade regulations on lights in fishing-boats. The story of this agitation belongs rather to the maritime history of England than to that of Newlyn—suffice it to say that partly in consequence of the representations of boat-owners here, and at other fishing ports, the regulations have been modified, according to the wishes of the fishermen. Several public meetings have been held, and Government enquiriés instituted on this subject during the past five years.

3.—The Newlyn Art Exhibition in 1876, when a number of curiosities were collected in the place and exhibited in Newlyn Town Reading-room (since transformed into a dwelling-house.) This exhibition, which was highly creditable to the town, may be regarded as the precursor to the energetic action of Newlyn folk in connection with the International Fisheries Exhibition of 1883, and of our present West Cornwall Fisheries Exhibition of 1884. Several medals and prizes were taken by Newlyn exhibitors in the "Fisheries" of 1883.

4.—The road between Newlyn and Penzance, which had long been unsafe and unsatisfactory, having been practically destroyed by the storms of 1881, a new road and bridge was constructed and opened in 1883, which has shortened the distance between Penzance and Newlyn.

NEWLYN AS IT IS.

ST. PETER'S, NEWLYN.

The fishing town of Newlyn West is situated on the west side of Mount's Bay, nearly one mile from Penzance, and nine from the Land's End. The population was 3638 in 1881. There is a parish called Newlyn East, 40 miles distant, near Grampound.

The parish church of St. Peter's, erected in 1866, stands close to the river on the Tolcarn or eastern side. It has a chancel, nave, and north aisle with transept. The style is Early English, and is a good specimen of the adaptation of that style to the use of granite. The east window in the chancel is a fine representation of the crucifixion with other figures. Over the altar is the reredos of terra-cotta put up in 1884, representing the Last Supper, after the famous painting of Leonardo da Vinci.

The best view of the church is from the west door, which is nearly always open during the day. The church is "free and open," and weekly communion has been maintained there since its consecration, and a daily service, with few interruptions, for the last 12 years. The value of the benefice is £150, and a house.

On the north-west side of St. Peter's Church is the Vicarage, erected in 1877 by the present vicar, with its garden open to the river. On the opposite south-east side is the iron school-house, erected in 1881. The school has a class-room attached, used as an infant school.

Beside this school, on the Madron side of the river, there is, on the Paul side, the large Wesleyan school near the slip, and on the hill over Newlyn the handsome Board Schools erected in 1879.

Further up the river than the Vicarage is the lovely little estate of Zimmerman's Cot, now occupied by Mr. Curnow. In the garden, embosomed with woods and wood clad hills, one might almost fancy oneself in a clearing in a virgin forest, rather than within a couple of hundred yards of a street, and within a mile of the largest town in Cornwall. The scenery is more striking to ordinary West Cornish visitors as being so un-Cornish in type, the rich woodlands covering steep hills. The scene is more like a woody glen of Bohemia or the Rhine land, than in a well-cleared county like Cornwall.

There is an old Cornish granite cross near the vicarage, and also a mediæval archway.

TOLCARN.

Above the Vicarage is the picturesque pile of rocks or carn of Tolcarn, whence a beautiful view of Newlyn and the Bay may be easily obtained. On the elvan rocks of Tolcarn, net-like veins may be seen, about which a curious Cornish legend is told that "the Bucca-boo (probably the storm-spirit or the Cornish Neptune, though in the Middle Ages represented as the Devil) once was inclined to go a-fishing, and therefore got hold of the fishermen's nets at Newlyn. (Possibly a mythic way of saying, the storm carried away their nets.) Now some of these nets belonged to men in Paul choir. The Buccaboo, with the nets, was pursued by the choir chanting the Creed—to which he had a strong objection. On getting on the top of the hill, pursued by the Christian choir, he flew over the Coomb, and settling on Tolcarn, turned the nets into stone, where they may still be seen." (Possibly this is an allegory of the overcoming of heathenism by the Christian disciples of St. Pol-de-leon.)

Below "the Carn," or Tolcarn rather, is the Tolcarn Mills, where Blake's stone breaking machines may be seen, the property of Mr. Runnalls, an interesting application of water power. The mills are very picturesque, and have been made the subject of paintings by artists visiting the place. It may be worth mentioning that many parts of Newlyn have appeared in the Royal Academy, the Salon at Paris, and other picture galleries, e.g.: The view in front of the Vicarage toward Zimmerman's Cot has been painted for the Salon, and the road to Newlyn Town for the Academy.

THE ROAD.

The shores of Mount's Bay around the Tolcarn inn, and between Tolcarn and Penzance, show the havoc effected by the Atlantic storms, mainly of 1880-82. A road formerly existed between here and Wherry Town which, however, for the last twenty years was occasionally washed by the sea during gales. This road itself once was a little inland, and grass land stood between it and the Bay, now it has been, as the traveller may notice —quite washed away by the Atlantic rollers. The encroachments of the sea in Mount's Bay are a difficult problem. Tradition, as we have seen, represents that Newlyn is a new town close to a portion of the Bay, where the sea destroyed an old town on the site where our proposed pier is being constructed in deep water, and that St. Michael's Mount once stood in a forest. These stories have been rejected, but are not without evidence in their favour, in the remains of trees, and even nuts found at very low tides under the shingle of Mount's Bay.

NEWLYN INSTITUTE.

In Street-an-Nowan, on the Paul or western side of the Newlyn river, the first place worth mentioning is the Newlyn Institute, close to the bridge, a humble but useful room where, for 3/- a year, the visitor may have the privilege of a reading-room, provided with the local and two London daily papers, the use of a small library, and games of drafts, chess, &c. There are lectures here in the winter in connection with the Institute, and also concerts and penny readings.

Opposite to the Institute, on the other side of the bridge, are the offices of the Mount's Bay Fishing Boats Mutual Insurance Club (registered under the Friendly Societies Act.)

Outside the Institute is an open space close to the sea, used for fish packing where, once or twice a year, generally about Corpus Christi Penzance fair, a sort of impromptu fair is got up for the entertainment of the juveniles. The scene here, after a catch of fish, is very striking. The crowds of carts ready to carry the finny treasures of the deep to the Great Western Railway station, the numerous packers busy placing the fish into boxes, baskets, or "fish pads," with broken ice to preserve them, the boats rowing ashore with their white cargoes of food, the shouting, bustle, and hurry of the scene are very striking to strangers, and full of picturesque elements.

THE ICE AND SMELTING WORKS.

The Gulval Ice Works are close by, and form an interesting sight for visitors. It is strange that the two chief sights, in the way of factories in Newlyn, belong to the extremes of heat and cold, *i.e.*, the Ice Works where the ice is pounded and packed with the fish to preserve for the London and other markets; and the Smelting Works of Stable Hobba, where tin is smelted for the mines. The latter establishment is well worth a visit, especially for those unaccustomed to smelting operations. The scene at noon and at 6 p.m., when the molten metal is poured out from the furnaces is very striking. The metal as it cools forms graceful stalactites, like icicles, over the glowing molten stream, of apparently liquid fire. This, though rarely visited, is one of the prettiest sights of Newlyn.

Near the Ice Works, a little beyond the Post Office, is an old dial plate, one of the few relics of old Newlyn. The inscription apparently of the age of Queen Anne is "Time flys *(sic.)* Death hastes, a moment may be wished, when worlds want wealth to buy."

A little further we come to the Wesleyan schools, a substantial building erected near the chapel. This chapel, in Jack Lane, is a commodious edifice built in 1834.

NEWLYN TOWN.

In Newlyn the most interesting building to the antiquary are (1) the curious old house with secret chamber and cellar, dated 1617, on the cliff, (2) the old houses in Primrose-court possibly of the end of the seventeeth century, and (3) the old Navy Inn, now a private dwelling-house. Cliff House is also a sample of a good Cornish house of the last century, when the gentry lived among the Newlyn people. Christ Church Mission, belonging to St. Peter's Church, is at the end of the Bowjey. It is licensed by the Bishop for Holy Communion and Baptisms. There is another Mission-room at the back of the Fisherman's Arms, belonging to the Church of England. The Primitive Methodists also have a chapel here.

THE OLD PIER.

The small pier, now purchased by the solicitor of the harbour commissioners, was erected, it seems, about the time of James I., and was long regarded as part of the Kenegie estate.

NEWLYN PIER.

The proposed pier is the greatest enterprise that has yet been conducted in connection with "the little fisher town" of Newlyn. It is a pier to be constructed from the Green Rocks, situated in the south of Newlyn, 760 feet long, composed of strong concrete walls filled with rubble. The first 400 feet of the pier are to be in an easterly direction, then there will be a slight deflection northward, so that the last 360 feet will be turned a little inward to the shore towards the north-east. At the end of the pier there will be a small lighthouse and bollards fixed at convenient distances. In addition to this it is proposed ultimately to put a northern pier, leaving the shore close to the river's mouth (on the west side of it) opposite the Newlyn Institute. These two piers, if completed, would make Newlyn harbour one of the safest harbours for small vessels (i.e., those that most need harbours for shelter) in the West of England. It would be sheltered, naturally, from the dominant "south-wester" (the most dangerous wind in our British seas,) from the north, north-west, and north-east, and artificially from the south and south-east. The easterly wind would be the only wind that could do harm in the harbour, and this is rarely violent or dangerous in these parts.

The Bill for the Provisional Order for the Newlyn pier was approved of by the Board of Trade, and has received the assent of both Houses of Parliament and also of Her Majesty. The other piers bracketted with Newlyn are Aldborough, Baltimore and Skibbereen, Carlingford, Lough, Chatham, Cromer, Cullen, Dawlish, Eyemouth, Fraserburgh, and Hove. Twenty-three commissioners have been appointed, in connection with the Act, as Newlyn Harbour Commissioners.

CHRONOLOGY OF NEWLYN.

Century XV.

Newlyn Pier built by Bishop Lacy	1435
Visit of William of Worcester, and description of Newlyn	1478
Visit of Perkin Warbeck to Mount's Bay	1497

Century XVI.

Landing by French on the Bay—burning of Marazion	1514
Lelands visit to Newlyn	1533
Suppression of Monasteries	1536
Cornish Rebellion	1549
Madron Register commences	1577
Spanish Armada off Mount's Bay	1588
Capture of Newlyn by the Spaniards, under Don Diego de Brochero. Town burnt	1595

Paul Register commences, the old one being burnt by the Spaniards.

Century XVII.

Carew's account of Newlyn	1602
Oldest house (?) now in Newlyn	1617
Old pier built about	1620
Fairfax sacks Penzance	1648
Daniel of Laregan nearly killed. Fighting at Penzance	1648
Restoration of Charles II.	1660
Visit of Queen Catherine of Braganza to Gwavas Lake	1661

Excitement in Cornwall about Bishop Trelawney	1687
Cornish offer services to William III ...	1688
First visit of John Wesley to Newlyn and first sermon there	1747
Second visit	1748
Third visit, complaint of want of discipline ...	1750
Fourth visit, storm during sermon, most remained	1751
Fifth visit, taken ill	1753
Sixth visit	1755
Seventh visit	1757
Eighth visit, storm	1760
Ninth visit	1762
Tenth visit, he complained of failing voice ...	1765
Eleventh visit, bad weather, but none left him	1766
Twelfth visit, "Surely God will have a people, even in this place	1768
Thirteenth visit	1770
Wesley's last sermon in Newlyn in the open air	1789
Death of John Wesley, aged 88	1791

Century XIX.

First census of Newlyn	1801
Battle of Trafalgar—mourning for Nelson ...	1806
First part of Sir John Moore's troops from Coruna land	1809
Peace rejoicings	1814
Rejoicings after Waterloo	1815
Great storm—the Green flooded, several houses in Newlyn washed away	1817
Newlyn boats begin Irish fishery ..	1826
Reform Bill—great excitement at election ...	1831

Wherrytown mine re-opened	1836
Queen Victoria and Prince Albert visited Mount's Bay—great rejoicing	1846

NEWLYN AS A SEPARATE PARISH.

St. Peter's Newlyn made a new Parish	1848
Prince Lucien Bonaparte's visit to Newlyn	1860
Monument to Dolly Pentreath in Paul	1860
St. Peter's Church built	1866
Order for a Newlyn pier obtained, but allowed to expire	1872
Death of Rev. J. Pope Vibert	1873
Induc. of present vicar, Rev. W. S. Lach-Szyrma	1874
British Archœlogical Congress Art Exhibition at Newlyn	1876
Centenary of Cornish language	1876
Erection of Newlyn vicarage	1877
Consecration of Archbishop Benson and restoration of Cornish diocese. First confirmation ever held in Newlyn	1877
Loss of the Malakoff	1879
Formation of "Mount's Bay Fishing Mutual Insurance Club"	1879
Newlyn Institute founded (in present form)	1881
Scheme for new pier renewed	1882
Blake's stone breaking machine fixed in Tolcarn mills	1882
New road from Newlyn to Penzance opened	1883
Fishery Exhibition and Bazaar for Newlyn pier	1884

CPSIA information can be obtained
at www.ICGtesting.com
Printed in the USA
248297LV00003B